Who Will You Be the Day After Yesterday?

Who Will You Be the Day After Yesterday?

Mark Pugh

Sovereign World

Sovereign World Ltd
PO Box 777
Tonbridge
Kent TN11 0ZS
England

ISBN 1 85240 418 3

The publishers aim to produce books which will help to extend and build up the Kingdom of God. We do not necessarily agree with every view expressed by the author, or with every interpretation of Scripture expressed. We expect each reader to make his/her judgement in the light of their own understanding of God's Word and in an attitude of Christian love and fellowship.

Cover design by CCD, www.ccdgroup.co.uk
Typeset by CRB Associates, Reepham, Norfolk
Printed in the United States of America

Contents

Foreword

There are those who think that today's Church has a choice between moving on or standing still. That is not true. The fact is we are all travelling into the future at the rate of sixty seconds a minute – that's fast! A Formula One racing driver once said, "At 200 mph you are covering a football field every second – it helps to know where you are going before you get there!"

Mark Pugh in *Who Will You Be the Day After Yesterday*? poses a question that needs to be addressed – and addressed now. As people move into adulthood they make a will in the event of their death – deciding the destination of their assets in the event of their demise. Too few consider "making a will for their life" examining their assets with a view to achieving their God-given destiny today.

A fortune teller once told her naïve client his supposed future with the words, "You'll be sad, miserable and poor until you are thirty."

"What happens at thirty?" he inquired.

"At thirty you will get used to it."

Mark Pugh is aware that there is a generation that refuses to "get used" to anything. They are people who are "Serious for God". They don't want just want change – they want to be part of the transformation that brings change about. This book is for them.

Marshall McCluhan once said, "Tomorrow is our permanent address." He was right.

John Glass
General Superintendent
Elim Pentecostal Churches

Introduction

We are living in times of great opportunity. God, right now is searching the earth, looking for those who will take these opportunities by the scruff of the neck and see total transformation in everything they are and everything they touch. You are one of the people He has earmarked to excel in this time – to be a world changer – both of your personal world and the world of other people. He has seen greatness in you. He whispers dreams in your heart, dreams of who you can be and what you can do and He hasn't given you the scent of these dreams to simply tantalize your senses, but to transform you.

Being chosen or appointed is so important. As eleven players walk onto the football pitch chosen by their manager, or as politicians stand in front of the cameras, picked by their political party, so you have been chosen, picked, nominated – call it whatever you like. You have been given the go-ahead from God. He's given you the nod, the thumbs up, the letter of approval which says you are in His plans to be a key child of His in the *Now generation.*

It is possible to miss God's call however. I have seen many of God's chosen nominees miss out. They could be living their dream, but they are not. Don't ignore the call. Don't take His nomination lightly. There are two things that can stop us being part of the *Now generation.* Our ***past*** and our ***future***, or our yesterdays and our tomorrows.

Yesterdays

Imagine you are in a room. It all looks very familiar. You have become very accustomed to your surroundings and each thing in the room is as it was the last time you looked. In one corner there is a dark shadow that represents something wrong you once did. You glance to the other side of the room and very quickly you are reminded of a painful incident that happened in your life. In fact, there are a number of things which remind you of your past and their memories make you feel like you are living with them still today.

I remember many of the hurts, disappointments, rejections and abuse that people have shared with me over my years of ministry. I remember the tears and feel the pain of many heartbreaking stories, wishing that none of them had happened. I'd love to pray a prayer that instantly removed the memory of all these things;

a prayer that would take them to an elevator in a corner of the room, walk them inside and press a button to transport them quickly from this floor of dark disappointment and shame, to the next floor of released hopes and dreams. Wouldn't it be great if we could, at the press of a button, find an automatic solution to our past?

Rather than placing us in an elevator, I find that God usually accompanies us up a staircase, step by step leading us into new things. He holds our hand and takes us to a place that is far beyond our expectations – a place of healing and wholeness rather than a place of pain; a place of freedom, rather than a place of restrictive captivity. He walks the steps of our journey with us. Each day when the sun shines through the window of our lives, our past is not meant to create a shadow that hangs over our aspirations. The sun is meant to bring light and hope for our journey. So many people have limited God from working in their lives because of their past. Yet the *Now generation* know the floor or level that they have lived on and experienced places no restrictions on the levels they will rise to. The doors are not locked, there are no guards keeping you in – your past cannot hold you. Who you are today does not need to reflect your yesterdays. Leave the past behind. Don't sit there hiding behind the pain of yesterday. See the light of Jesus bring hope into the room of your life and illuminate the stairway of healing where God wants to lead you to another level.

Tomorrow

Tomorrow never comes for some and they don't want it to come either. It is far easier to start something tomorrow. Whether it is getting down to study for an exam, begin a fitness plan, or make a change in your behaviour, the intention of tomorrow can help appease the conscience without the inconvenience of change. It can make a person feel well-intentioned and hopeful, but sadly can produce a self-defeated, low level of satisfaction in a person's life as they constantly fail to achieve what they would like. Dreamers can be a bit like that, but I must admit I love to spend time with them. Dreamers are people who think and talk about things that could be or even should be! There are many people who can easily commentate on the present state of the world and predict the bleakness of the future, but I love it when people manage to lift their sights above the cesspit of cynicism and see what could be. *But the **Now generation** will not be content with projecting these hopes continuously into the future, they want to see them in the present.*

I believe that such dreamers are longing for others to come alongside them – to believe in them and to encourage and assist them in whatever way they can, in order to turn their dreams into realities. If I believe the future is going to be great then I want to do all I can to turn that hope into a present reality. I wonder what dreams are in your heart? I wonder which ones constantly cry out from within, longing to be heard and to surface above the accepted norm? Turn your reality into the stuff of dreams. Dreams cannot continue to be dreams – they must become reality. If they don't become reality then they become disappointments. The future hopes you perceive must become your present experience. God is looking for people who will rise up and move from dreaming the dream to living the dream. It is within your grasp and you can hold it in your hands. He will give you great boldness, courage, persistence and energy to make it happen. Sadly some prefer to "sleep the dream", rather than to "live the dream". Avoid dying a dreamer at all costs. Wake up, get out of your comfortable bed and start doing something about your dreams. Don't just lie there – live it!

Yesterdays . . .

When I go to the cinema, I'm often directed as to where I can and cannot go by what looks like a few poles on stands with lengths of seatbelts trailed from one to another. I would have no problem in climbing over them or even doing a limbo underneath them. I could even just detach one of the ends and ignore their subtle pleas for obedience without any difficulty. But why do I comply with these instructions when it would be so simple to ignore them? Perhaps it's because I believe they have a right to be there. No one has ever explained this to me, but somehow I have calculated that they are there for a reason and I have no right to challenge them.

In our lives there are many such barriers that we submit to simply because they are there. These barriers keep us confined to a certain place or on a certain level. I'm convinced that our enemy has bought a job lot of these barriers and placed them strategically at the stairways of possibilities in our lives. God has already put the next levels of life in place for us, complete with stairways to get there, but Satan comes along and erects a barrier, so we assume it must mean "No Entry".

Recently, I was at a youth camp and made my early morning dart to one of the shower blocks on site. Each morning as I lay on my airbed listening to my neighbours sizzling bacon, I felt motivated to get to the showers before the big queues started. It worked every morning except on this particular occasion. As I approached, I noticed a queue of guys outside the male cubicles. As much as I loathe standing in a line and waiting for something, I thought I would make the most of my predicament and engage in some meaningful conversation with my fellow pre-showered line-standers. The queue got bigger as we anticipated one of the five shower cubicle doors opening, and no doubt we were each playing our own version of "10 green bottles" subconsciously in our minds. A door opened, and a wet-haired man emerged in a cloud of steam like someone walking onto the "Stars in Your Eyes" stage. As he walked past, smelling of the latest shower gel he wryly acknowledged the now lengthy queue, and the young guy at the front clutched the towel which was previously draped over his shoulder and speedily made his way to his water rendezvous, looking overly excited for someone on a youth camp. The rest of us continued in conversation for some time and then a question dawned on me, "Is there actually anyone in the four other cubicles?" I sheepishly moved towards one of the doors and gave it a gentle push. Door 1 opened and revealed an empty cubicle. Door 2 the same, in fact doors 3 and 4 were the same also! Groans of disbelief went up from the gathered, patient line of sweat-smelling campers and a rush for the empty cubicles ensued. I had assumed "No Entry" because others had assumed the same, but the reality was very different. There are times when we simply assume there is a "No Entry" sign blocking the stairways of opportunity in our lives and that the dreams of the future are impossible, just because we have followed others who have considered them inaccessible. But we must go and try the door and not just accept the appearance of a barrier! The enemy regularly tries to put barriers and obstacles in our way, but they are illegitimate, have no real significance in our lives, and certainly cannot stop us moving to another level. Let's look at some of these barriers together.

Barriers of our own failures

If you were sat in a large gathering of Christians and the speaker said that God was about to reveal who was the worst Christian in the building, in all probability a fairly large section of the people in the meeting would begin to panic, certain that the speaker was referring to them.

I wonder if you would be one of them? The reality is that each of us has failures in our lives, and whether they are present or past, they can cause us to carry a heavy weight of unworthiness around on our shoulders and make us feel like the lowest of the low. This alone can convince us that we are not "good enough" and that there is a barrier stopping us rising to new levels.

I know that I am not good at a number of things. The reason I don't volunteer my striking services to the local football team is the same reason why I don't apply for the chef's job when I see a restaurant advertising for a new member of staff – I'm not good enough at the skills required. But even though God does not accept us on the basis of our being highly-skilled or talented or clever, this is exactly the reason that many people don't offer their services to God – they simply don't feel they are good enough.

In all of my years of education I only ever scored one goal when playing football. I was nine years of age, in the school playground with goals posts made out of sweaters. There was no crowd watching and I doubt whether anyone else remembers it. I remember it clearly though, as my mates jumped with joy and ruffled their hands through my hair in a congratulatory way. In truth the goal was a bit of a fluke, but I played "out of my skin" for the rest of that game. I had connected with an inner belief that I could do this. I chased every ball, went for every shot and was transformed from a person who groaned when people took the risk of passing the ball to me, to a shouting, hollering player who wanted everyone to give me the ball. If the enemy can get us to believe we are not good enough then we will stand around on the edges, avoiding the real action.

I have a problem ...

I remember when I started to learn to drive. On one of my first lessons the instructor took me onto a busy dual carriageway road. That meant I could put my foot down a little more and get used to a bit of speed. As I approached a roundabout I gently applied my foot to the brake and came to a stop because a car travelling in the opposite direction looked like he was going to travel around the circumference of the roundabout. As I patiently waited for him to continue driving past the exit where I was sat, something happened which gave me my first personal taste of road rage. This driver didn't drive past my exit; he actually came off at the exit before. I began to think of the lack of respect he had shown me and other motorists, as he didn't bother indicating to tell us what he was doing. I know it sounds quite sad, but it really annoyed me. After all, I only stopped at the junction because he gave me the impression I needed to. I could actually have carried on safely onto the roundabout and avoided the embarrassment of stalling the car and clunking into first gear. I was so mad that as I pulled off (kangaroo petrol included) and drove around the roundabout, I ranted a little to my instructor about how bad it was that the guy hadn't indicated. His response was a killer! He said, "You mean just like you did then?" I was so fixated with the failures of the other driver that I didn't notice my own! I had just done exactly the same thing – gone across the roundabout and not indicated. I could see someone else's errors but not my own.

We are in this together!

I make mistakes, I get it wrong, I fail, I mess up and I've made some right muck ups! I'm not just referring to breaking the Highway Code, but failing God's code. We've all done it.

> *"For all have sinned and fall short of the glory of God."* (Romans 3:23)

Don't try to deny or run away from your failings – you must face them. Most homes have at least one area that is unofficially designated as the "junk area". It may be called the storage cupboard or the attic, but essentially it is the place where people put stuff they no longer use. Whenever I have visitors to my home, I never show them my junk area. I don't want them to see the messy and unorganized parts of my home. I want to keep it hidden from their view. But that is often how we approach God. We sing our songs, say our prayers, invite Him to sit with us and even tell Him to make Himself at home – but we'll not mention the junk room. Listen, He knows all about it and wants to help sort it out. Having a junk room only becomes a barrier to progress in our lives if it is hidden. Recently I had a good sort through some of the junk in my home. Most of the things I was able to put into special bags and leave at the bottom of my drive for collection by a local charity. If I hadn't faced up to the junk it would have still been in the house, but because I was willing to face it, someone else was able to help deal with it.

That is exactly how it is with God. If we hide our sin and don't deal with it, we will find the junk areas of our lives getting more and more messy. If we face it, Jesus offers to take it away. The junk of your past can be removed from your life and you can know a totally clean start, free from barriers and limitations. I want God to be able to really make Himself at home in my life. Rather than putting locks on junk cupboard doors to keep Him, out I want to invite Him to help me sort them out.

The psalmist David wanted this when he said,

> *"Search me, O God, and know my heart;*
> *test me and know my anxious thoughts."*
> (Psalm 139:23)

He wasn't saying "Hey, search me!" in an arrogant way, believing that God would find nothing wrong. David knew that he wasn't perfect, but he didn't want his junk to be hidden – he wanted it to be exposed. He knew that the greatest friend of sinners is God. He knew that Jesus is the one who offers the greatest hope when we feel shame and that He would help him highlight and deal with offensive ways in his life.

Are you ready to ask God to search you? Maybe there are failures in your life that you've locked away so tightly that you believe they will always be there no matter what. If I could shout on the pages of this book at this point you would hear a very loud "NO!!!" Don't live with your failures! Jesus gave His life on the cross to deal with the mess we have made. Ask the greatest friend of sinners to help you clear out your junk rooms and let Him take them away.

> *"If we confess our sins, he is faithful and just and will forgive us our sins and purify us from all unrighteousness."* (1 John 1:9)

Shame on me ...

You can't *change* the past, but you can have it dealt with and you can stop living under a cloud of shame. It's almost like we have created a time-travelling machine in our minds that keeps thinking back to moments of personal shame. We picture the scene, recreate the moment, experience a resurrection of the emotions we felt then, only to discover that we can't change it. We leave with a reinforced sense of shame.

I was always under the impression that one of the advantages of CDs replacing vinyl records was that they don't scratch. However, I've subsequently discovered that they do scratch. I was at a church recently where they were playing a gentle worship CD as people were making their way into the service, when all of a sudden a scratch meant that the CD kept jumping back and forth very quickly over a very small fraction of music. This gentle environment began to sound like a rave and I wondered how people would respond. The sound engineer, obviously experienced in this phenomenon, banged the CD player and it quickly skipped over the scratch and began playing the gentler tones of respectable, sanctified sounds again. I've spent time with people who have tried the same approach when their mind gets stuck on a past shameful memory – they bang themselves on the head! In fact they keep banging themselves on the head. It never does any good, but it can make us feel like we are at least punishing ourselves for our past mistakes.

Many of the shameful things that people carry around with them are things they feel they can't talk about, because people would be shocked and horrified if they knew. (One of the least discussed issues for Christians is that of sexual temptations and struggles.) Over the years I have had the honour of listening to many people's stories. There have been times when some of these people have struggled to say what they really wanted to say. They talk about everything except the thing they are really struggling with. I have tried to help them by sharing some of my own struggles and issues in the area that I have a hunch they are wanting to talk about. Sometimes you would have thought that Elvis had just walked in the room – such was the look of disbelief on their faces. Some had been carrying their shame alone for so long, they were convinced they were the only person facing that issue. When they discovered that many people struggled with it, a great weight was lifted off them.

I want you to know that whatever you are struggling with, or however you have failed in the past, you are not alone. I believe that trying to hide our failures and struggles can be as damaging as the failure itself. God will forgive the sin and take it away from our lives, but if we still visit the shame, then each time we attempt to move to another level we will be confronted by that shameful barrier holding us back. You can overcome this barrier alone. Find someone you trust – confess your shame and begin to know a release from its hold on you.

> *"Confess your sins to each other and pray for each other so that you may be healed."* (James 5:16)

He goes on and on ...

I have absolutely no desire to pay any compliments to the devil, but I must concede there is something that he is good at. He's brilliant at accusing us about bad things we have done. He's not generally daft enough to make up fictitious accusations, but he takes things we have done and said, and uses them to make us feel failures.

> *"For the accuser of God's people brings accusations before God both day and night."*
> (Revelation 12:10 paraphrase)

They may be things that happened ten years ago, or ten minutes ago. He has absolutely no interest in how long ago it was and he is not that bothered about what you did. All he is concerned with is stealing your effectiveness, and stopping you from being an active part of the *Now generation* by placing a barrier before you to stop you moving on in God. There can be times when his whispers seem deafening. Every time we try to move to another level in God he comes along with an accusation that is meant to stop us in our tracks and make us turn back. He cannot bear to face the realities of today – which is the reality of a new day. Your story of sin is now God's story or His-story. You have given Him your sin and He has given you His perfect righteousness. This is the deal of all time – I gave Him my home-made filthy rags and He gave me His perfect designer gear. The Bible says that as far as the east is from the west, that is how far God has removed our failures and rebellion from us (Psalm 103:12). If you were to travel north you would get to the North Pole. By taking one more step further you would begin to travel south. You can measure the distance between north and south. But if you walk east, you keep walking east. You never get to an east pole – it doesn't exist. The east goes on and on. The same is true of the west and because they both go on and on, you can't measure the distance between them. That is how far God has removed our shame from us. When the devil whispers malicious reminders into our minds, remind him of the truth that you are now in a new day and that the sin he is referring to, no longer belongs to you.

All been paid for . . .

I remember hearing in the news of a lady who had received an astronomical electrical bill for her home. Apparently the electricity company's computer program had gone wrong and a considerable number of noughts were added to what should have been the correct amount. A bill for £120 had become a bill for £120 million. There was no way she was going to pay it. In fact there was no way she could pay it. The company involved apologised, rectified the problem and sent out the correct bill much to the relief of the lady concerned.

The Bible teaches us that each person is accumulating a massive bill, which is going to land at the door of their lives. There will be no mistakes in the calculations of this outstanding amount however, and there will be no right to appeal. The invoice will list each wrong thing that the person has done and said, plus those things which they have thought. No matter how long or how short the list, the final balance due will be considerably higher than anyone can afford to pay. The Bible says that the full payment for sin is death, in other words, an eternal separation from God. One of the most hated punishments

I would face as a child when I misbehaved was being sent to my room. Time used to go so slowly as I sat on my bed, convinced I was missing out on something more exciting downstairs. Well, imagine spending all of eternity – forever and ever – in a place of punishment, knowing that you are missing out on enjoying the greatest place to be. That is what it will be like for those who at the end of life on this earth are confronted with the invoice for their sin, with the words, "final demand – payment due immediately". This will not be the case for those of us who know Jesus and have received His forgiveness. The bill has already been paid by Him and the reality of heaven is a dead cert for us.

A few years ago I was trying to be all romantic by ordering some very nice flowers from a local florist for my wife to be delivered on Valentine's Day. The florist's shop had no car park, but the local pub did, and as it was only 9 am in the morning it was deserted. I parked up, locked the car and proceeded to make my way to the flower shop. I must have only been there about ten minutes, but as I started to make my way back to the car, feeling very good about my romantic gesture, I noticed two very big and mean looking guys standing either side of my car. They had attached an ugly wheel clamp to one of my wheels and were insisting on an extortionate amount of money in order to release my car and prevent them from towing it away. I was gutted.

They pointed to some signs high up on the lamp posts which I had not noticed and I knew these guys did not understand the art of negotiating. They were serious about wanting payment and I was serious about wanting my car back. I had to pay up, and although I had enough money on me, it was money that was allocated to other things. I had to use it to get my car back, but incredibly in the next few days, someone gave me the money to cover the payment. Really, I was at fault and I owed the bill, but someone was kind enough to pick up the cost. I was so pleased, but I am so much more in awe of Jesus who gave His life to pay the bill for my sin. More than freeing my car, He has freed my heart and conscience.

> *"It is for freedom that Christ has set us free."*
> (Galatians 5:1)

I am free from my past, can enjoy life in the present, and will know the incredible experience of being with Him for eternity.

These barriers of failure, inadequacy, shame and accusations are not legitimate restrictions. God has made it possible for you to ignore their appeals for your obedience and to move up to new levels. Move forward now. They have held you back long enough. It is now time for a new day in your life.

Barriers of other people's failures

We may have taken responsibility for our own failings, but what about times when others fail us? I'm not talking of someone who forgot to return your CD, but failures that have resulted in our harm. This can be all the more difficult to take when the person who hurts us has been a close friend, colleague, or family member. I have met people who find it so difficult to get past these hurts. They want to move on to higher levels, but the barrier of hurts just continually seems to stop them in their tracks. As with our own failures, denial is not the way forward. Pretending the hurt does not exist is just not real, and God is totally for reality. It is really important to remember that while the hurt may be real, it doesn't need to be a barrier. Nothing that has happened in our past has the right to hold us back.

Round and round and round we go ...

If someone has hurt you then you have probably been a victim. This doesn't mean though, that you should walk around the rest of your life with a bull's-eye on your forehead, expecting that people will always take shots at you. There is a funny incident I remember when I was probably a little insensitive as a pastor. One of the guys in my youth group had been walking home from work when a car slowed down next to him, wound down the window, and threw an open bottle of Tipex correction fluid at him. He told me the story in response to my question later that night, as to why he had white marks all over his face and in his hair. This had obviously been a traumatic thing for him, as it would for anyone who experienced such abuse. But all my years of learning sensitivity seemed to desert me as I could feel an irrepressible belly laugh rising up inside, and I heard myself say the words, "You must realize that you are *not* a mistake!" Thankfully we had the sort of friendship which was able to handle my humour and we both were able to turn it into a bit of a laugh.

Should he have allowed this incident to change his life? Maybe he should decide never to walk home again? Maybe he should wear a balaclava so that next time he is prepared? Maybe he was at fault? Maybe he should have walked on the other side of the road? Maybe he shouldn't have worn such a bright coat? The problem with asking these sorts of questions is, where do they stop? Asking questions can be a really good thing, but when we keep asking the same questions over and over again, we begin to go around in circles. These "circles" will hold us back and stop us moving forward. You may have been a victim of your past, but if you continually circumnavigate the issues in your present, you will develop a victim mindset. If you keep walking around something, it becomes by default the central thing in your life. Instead, you can move on.

Accept that some questions won't get answered this side of eternity

If you can't get an answer regarding issues in your life that are troubling you and holding you back, or at least can't get an answer you can understand, remind yourself that eternity will cast a light on things that we can't comprehend in this world. This is tough. We live in a world that demands answers and people will make them up if they can't find them out legitimately. Your questions are far too important to have made-up answers. God is totally for truth and if we leave our unanswered questions with Him, we can be sure that there will be no deceit or fabrication. He will preside over the truthful answer and will keep it safe until the time when He knows best to release it to us. So if you find yourself going round in circles, asking the same questions, just ask God one more time, but add the following to your enquiry:

> "Dear God, if you choose not to answer my questions at this point in my life, then help me to

leave them with You. I ask that You will give me the peace and grace to accept this and move on to another level in my life."

How to forgive the seemingly unforgivable

"I want to forgive him and I've asked God to help me, but every time I see him I get so angry . . . "

I recently watched a film that revolved around the main character having her memories of a relationship removed. If such procedures were possible, then I'm sure there would be huge waiting lists as people desperately tried to remove the recollections of painful moments and bad incidents. Our understanding and hopes for forgiveness can be as equally dramatic. We hope that if we close our eyes tight enough and pray for long enough, then our memory will be erased and we will feel fine next time we see the perpetrator of the hurt. We get so disappointed when we find that this is not the reality. I've heard so many people say the words, "I want to forgive but I can't".

What do they mean when they say they can't? They usually are referring to not being able to forget, or not being able to change their feelings. While they may not be able to do these things, it doesn't mean that they can't forgive. Forgiveness is about a conscious choice, a choice to make a break from the hurts of the past and not live each day facing the consequences. Forgiveness is about handing the issue over to God and leaving the outcome with Him.

A few years ago we owned a house that we couldn't sell. We had moved to another part of the country already, so we couldn't live in it either. We decided to rent it out. The only problem was, our tenant woke up one morning and decided that he was no longer going to pay for the privilege of living there. It took us some time to get him to leave, and the end result was a house he had trashed and a large debt that he hadn't paid. I was advised that there are companies who buy debts. It sounded a bit crazy to me, but when I looked into it I found out how it worked. Basically this guy was legally bound to owe me money – he had a legitimate bill that was outstanding. One of these debt-buying companies would offer to pay me an amount less than the debt in exchange for them being the new legal owners of the outstanding amount. They would then chase the debtor and attempt to reclaim the full amount. It was an option I didn't take in the end, but it did give me a picture of how forgiveness works. God has offered to manage any debts that are owing to us. If we hand them over to Him, then He takes the responsibility to do the right thing with them. We relinquish the right to chase payment ourselves and we make no claims against the person who has hurt us. We release it totally into God's hands to do whatever

He sees as right. We won't chase Him about it and we won't disagree with the way He handles it. We totally and completely let it go. We don't necessarily forget, and the person who hurt us may not be top of our Christmas card list, but we release them into God's care, Who handles all things with justice, righteousness and love.

Forgiveness doesn't undermine or question the severity or your hurt, but it releases you to be free from chasing a debt that you will never be able to satisfy. The act of forgiveness places God at the centre rather than our hurt. Are there people you need to release to God right now? Why not use the following prayer to help:

> "Dear God, I thank You that You forgave me of all the wrong that I have done. You know that I have been hurt by __________. Today I give You the debt that has been owed to me and I ask You to take charge of it. I leave this matter now in Your hands and trust You to handle it and do whatever You see as the right thing. As I release __________, I ask that You will fill me with Your love, healing and peace."

Not wanted ...

There is something within us that really wants to fit in. One of the most difficult responses we experience from others is that of being rejected. To feel like we are being pushed away can be so painful, it eats away at our sense of self-worth and value. We assume that if others don't want us, they have obviously weighed up our value and have found us lacking. One of the experiences I used to dread in school was the moment when the games teacher would get us all to line up against the wall and then choose two team captains, who would in turn select the most wanted players for their football team. The coin would be tossed and the winner would go first, choosing the most gifted and talented player. Then the other captain would choose the second best player, before nodding to the other captain to hand the initiative back over to him to select his second player and so on. This would go on for what seemed like an eternity as one by one, those who stood around me moved into their teams. I knew I would get picked eventually, but only because it was necessary that everyone played! I knew that if the captain had the ability to refuse to take a player then I would be a strong candidate to experience this option! After a year or so of this happening, I began to realize that this would be a repetitive script that would be well rehearsed. Then an answer came along. I had the misfortune of having an in-growing toenail. It really hurt and was a total pain and inconvenience, but it did mean that I didn't have to suffer the rejection of being lined up in front of the firing squad. I was pleased for an excuse to reject myself. Rather than other people telling me that I wasn't "up to the job", I would write myself off. It seemed such a good answer and one that I employed for some time.

I have seen other people do this so many times in life. They get so used to the rejection of others that they begin to find reasons to write themselves off, before anyone else can. The amazing thing about my circumstance was that I could have gotten my toenail treated with medical attention. People even offered to pray that God would heal it. I didn't want anyone's healing hands touching my problem though. If my toenail was sorted, then I would once again be exposed to the rejection of others. Many of the rejected people I meet have "toenail trouble" which they don't really want fixed. It may manifest itself in a bad attitude that is angry or critical, which says, "I'm going to make sure I reject myself before you do." It is the emotionally dark world of pre-emptive strikes that come out of our experiences of rejection.

You may have been rejected by a friend or a family member. Maybe even a parent you haven't seen for years, or by a person in authority. It's painful and it hurts. The feelings of standing against that cold and lonely wall while everyone else seems to be accepted as the "in-crowd" can feel like a dagger piercing your heart. When this happens, there are two things you must do:

1. Remind yourself that your value comes from God. Others may misjudge or misunderstand your value. But their rejection is based on their misjudgement of you, rather than on *who you really are*. God knows you are fantastic! It doesn't matter how much you or anyone else tries to convince Him otherwise. He is totally taken with you and this will never change.
2. Live up to the value that God has placed on you. Don't withdraw, or develop attitudes that will demean you, or do yourself down. Treat yourself with respect and value.

As we begin moving towards the staircase for another level in our lives, the barrier of rejection tells us that the journey is not worth taking. It tries to convince us that it will only end in disappointment. It will tell you that someone will be at the top of the stairs, shaking their head and motioning with their hands for you to turn around and go back to where you started. I can't promise that you will never be rejected again, but I can promise that the rejection you have experienced has no right to hold you back if you choose to move to new levels. Move forward with courage. Walk hand in hand with God, because He will never leave you or reject you. As you walk past the barriers and scale the stairway, hear His whispers of love and healing bringing value and purpose into your life.

Tomorrows ...

When do our aspirations for that "one-day" in the future become *this day*? When do people stop working towards that "dream career" and actually start experiencing it? When do our aspirations to be that man or woman of God change into reality? When does our prophetic vision become our tangible sight? When does tomorrow become today?

There is nothing in our yesterdays which disqualifies us from living the dreams of the future. You can push through the barriers of your past and see the dreams of tomorrow stand before you. However, they can look daunting, intimidating and far off. The dreams of the future can appear like a vast horizon that we view from a high cliff top – we can see it clearly, but it seems totally inaccessible. God doesn't give us the view of these dreams and then make it impossible for us to reach them. I don't hold up a bag of sweets in front of my kids, wave them around, show them the colour, describe the taste and then put them out of their reach. God doesn't allow us to see a vision of our dreams and then place them beyond us. You can reach them, but you must step out and walk towards them. There are barriers that will seek to discourage you from doing so, but you can press on beyond them.

Barriers of misunderstanding God's will

Where should I live? Who should I marry? What career should I choose? These and many more questions are often asked by those who desire to do God's will. There is often a real caution expressed by Christians when making decisions, because they don't want to miss out on God's plans for them and they don't want to make a mistake. This caution can create barriers which hold us back and these often come from a misunderstanding of who God is and how He works.

He's out to fail me!

Just before I took my first driving test, I read a book that aimed to prepare people for such an experience. Not having taken a test before and not knowing what to expect, I was relieved to read the book's explanation of what sort of people driving examiners are. I had previously constructed a stereotype that painted an image of a miserable-faced, unfeeling type of character whose only happy thought over breakfast would come from the prospect of failing lots of people during the day ahead. How comforted I was to read that this is far from the truth. It stated that I should expect a professional but happy person who really wanted to help me pass my test in order to make my life more complete. As I sat nervously in the waiting room of the test centre, these words brought some comfort. That was until I heard a booming voice call my name. The man I saw obviously hadn't read the book and the author of the book obviously hadn't met him. I was convinced he was out to fail me before I had even started. I know many Christians who have believed that God calls their name in a similar fashion. They believe that He is out to fail them before they have even begun to follow His instructions. Not surprisingly, it all went wrong for me that day. I was so convinced that I was starting out on this test with a minus score, that it caused me to be nervous and consequently to make quite a number of mistakes. Within a few minutes of being with him, my good sight had failed to correctly read a number plate, I stalled the engine a few times before pulling onto the road, and my emergency stop almost caused an accident. I failed, but from the moment I saw this ogre, I was convinced this would be the outcome.

God however, is not out to fail us. The Bible says that He is for us. Furthermore, we read that, *"If God is for us, who can be against us?"* (Romans 8:31).

Do you know that God *smiles* over you, even rejoices with excitement? He is in a very good mood! He wants you to "pass" with flying colours and even when you fail, He stands by you, encouraging you to try again.

But, if you believe that God is out to fail you, it will do one of two things:

1. **You won't try** ... Why turn up for an exam that you know the teacher will fail you on? Why go for a job interview when you know the interviewer doesn't want you to get the job? Why reach out to the dreams of your future horizon if you believe that God is hoping you fail? Why put yourself through the whole thing when you are resisting the inclinations of the Almighty? God isn't like this and He wants you to step out into the dreams He has placed within your heart.
2. **Your motivation will be to prove Him wrong** ... There have been many well-known sporting, acting and political personalities who have been driven by taunting words from the opposition or their enemies. A desire to make their critics "eat their words" has driven them to discipline, hard work and sacrifice. I don't want to spend my life believing that I need to prove God wrong. To live my life with this as a central aim would be a sure way of putting distance between us. I want to get closer to Him, not move away. In fact, getting closer to God is more important than any dream, desire, vision or ambition.

God is for you. He doesn't poke His tongue out at us and say "I told you so" when we fail. He comforts us, restores us, builds us up and whispers words of affirmation into our spirits. He is the coach at the side of the running track shouting "You can do it." He is the dad at the side of the football pitch cheering his kid on with every touch of the ball that they get. I love watching my kids take part in school performances. My wife and I are there early, queuing for the best seats, with a video recorder in one hand and a camera in the other. It may not be Hollywood but it is my daughter and son. I'm so proud of them and irrespective of whether they get all the words right or not, I'm encouraging them with an eager smile. Any friends or family who visit our house over the coming months are subjected to the home video, because we want to display our pride in our kids. If there was ever someone who was really proud of us and wanted us to succeed in life it is God. He is for you and He's with you to help you pass!

Waiting to hear Him speak

Have you ever listened to someone tell a story of how God spoke to them and wondered why God speaks so clearly to others when you struggle to hear anything? I have at times felt very intimidated by this, assuming that the volume of God's voice must be relative to the level of my spirituality. My desire to hear an audible voice message from God is never more apparent than when I am looking to understand and step out into my dreams. I would love to hear some confirmation that the thoughts and ideas I have are acceptable to God, but I never seem to hear His voice audibly. I have friends, who at points in their life, have heard Him speak in this way, but this form of communication seems to be more the exception than the rule. The Bible clearly says that, *"My sheep listen to my voice"* (John 10:27) and any relationship that is growing must have good communication. So how does He communicate with us?

Text messages

The car that I drive comes with a handbook. If I wanted to know how to do a routine thing with the car, like opening the bonnet or locking the glove compartment, I refer to the manual. The manufacturers do not anticipate that they need to speak to everyone about such matters, so they write it down so that it is clear and understood. God has done the same. The Bible is God's text message or handbook to us. There are no wasted words and no spam, and our response does not require us to call a very expensive phone number. I know that some of the Bible can be quite a challenge to understand, but it is God's message to us. It will always be right, will never change, and is what we use to measure whether our dreams, visions and prophetic words are in line with God's will or contrary to it. He will never say anything to us that contradicts what He has already written.

Voicemail

"You have 1 new message, sent today at 10.30am. To hear this message don't press 7, but go to church." God uses others to help us understand what God is saying. Preachers often get people coming up to them at the end of a service saying, "God really spoke to me this morning." God uses others as His mouthpiece to communicate His plans and purposes to us.

Chat rooms

There have been so many times where God has inspired or confirmed a plan with me through conversation with others. I love to be in a room of people who are sharing dreams at a heart level. The Bible says that we sharpen each other and help protect one another.

Relational understanding

I have been married quite a number of years now and very often I will know what my wife's thoughts would be on a particular issue before we have even discussed it. I can imagine her facial expressions and hear her words clearly in my mind as I anticipate what her response will be. In growing relationships people develop this kind of knowledge of one another. It is a part of intimacy. God wants us to know Him intimately, and the more we get to know Him, the more we begin to understand how He thinks and what He desires.

Hearing His voice above the noise of life

The reality is that God *does speak to us* and I think it would be fair to say that He speaks more often than we hear. It may or may not be audible and it doesn't really matter what method He uses. The important thing is that we hear Him. We are surrounded by sounds that we don't hear and sights that we don't see. Constantly there are digital, radio, TV, phone signals surrounding us, all carrying some form of sound or image. How do we hear and see these messages? We need the appropriate receivers – without them we have nothing with which to retrieve these signals and communicate them to our senses. There are times when we have the equipment, but it is not switched on. There are thousands of people walking around with bluetooth capacity phones who don't really know what it does or how it can be activated. The same can apply to Christians – we carry around the capability to hear God's voice but are not tuned in.

I'm always amazed when I see a football manager standing at the edge of the dugout, shouting instructions to his players on the other side of the field. There may be more than 30,000 other people shouting and singing in the stadium, and yet the boss's voice seems to get heard. The players have obviously found a way of tuning in. It may mean that they regularly look to the boss to see whether he is trying to say something and then when they realize he is, they tune in. Similarly, we need to regularly look to God, expectant that He may want to speak with us. We then tune in our thoughts, impressions, gut instincts and desires to receive a message from Him. I wonder if you recognize that within your life, God has already been speaking to you? Are there dreams and desires that are sitting in your heart, but you are unsure where they have come from? I have known people who have had dreams and desires for their lives, but because they are not sure if they are in God's will, they have hidden them for years. They await further instructions and place their dreams on a shelf like a study textbook that may be required at a later date. I believe that right now God may be speaking to you. He longs for us to impact our world with Jesus and I have found that He often uses the dreams that are within us to make this happen. If we shelve them, they won't do it. If we dream them they won't do it. The only way our dreams can impact our world is when we live the dreams. But how do we know if the dreams and desires in our lives are from God or us?

These boots were made for walking – the path of righteousness

I remember a few years ago when the aerial on our roof was moved by a violent storm. It was not pointing in the right direction and this resulted in our TV being unable to pick up the correct signal. If our lives are not facing the right direction then we are less likely to pick up God's communication and more likely to hear all the anti-God messages which are constantly being broadcast by society. We face God by walking a pathway of righteousness, or living out of a desire to please Him. We face away from God by following the selfish and corrupt desires in our lives and adhering to the rebellious attitudes of the world. If the destination is God, the pathway to Him is righteousness. It is living, breathing, desiring, working towards God, and thinking in a way that will please Him.

Most of us are very accustomed to travel now, but it wasn't that along ago, when as a young lad, the only time my family really travelled was to our holiday destination each year. I remember that it felt like the holiday began the moment I sat in the packed car, surrounded by bags and pillows, with an endless supply of snacks and sweets, which I think was my parent's way of trying to keep us relatively quiet on the journey. I loved the journey. With the familiarity of travel that we have today though, it is not unusual to perceive the journey as something that must be endured in order to get to where we want to go. We've lost the "joy of the journey" and if we are not careful, this can become an attitude, which is translated into our Christian walk. We must learn to look out of the window and enjoy the things we pass on the way. I regularly say to stressed-out couples that are meticulously planning their big wedding day that they must make the most of the journey. They will (hopefully) never pass the same way again and they must take time to stop and appreciate all that they are doing. As we head towards the destination of eternity let's remember that we are on a great journey. If our hearts are open and desiring to be right with God then the promise of the Bible is that God will ensure that He guides our steps.

> *"A man's steps are directed by the LORD."*
>
> (Proverbs 20:24)

For us to discern whether the dreams in our heart are from God or ourselves it is crucial that we are walking a pathway of righteousness and enjoying our daily walk with God. If we are facing the right direction then we will pick up the communication of the Holy Spirit who will help us discern what is from God and what is not.

Desires of the heart

"Delight yourself in the LORD
and he will give you the desires of your heart."
(Psalm 37:4)

The desires and dreams that sit in our hearts are like sparks of destiny. They are trying to catch alight by grabbing our attention in order to set our lives passionately on fire with purpose. Not all our desires are good though. We read that our heart is *"deceitful above all things"* (Jeremiah 17:9) and this gives us the ability to have desires, which are sinful. We need to constantly be on our guard against such desires and keep our feet walking towards God.

What desires do you have in your heart? If you are walking a path of righteousness and open to hearing God's voice, then the probability is that the dreams within you are planted by God. They are constantly creating imaginative sparks within you, bustling for your attention, longing for the day when they will grow up into a proper fire. These dreams are really precious. Others may not see them or even understand them. We only have to think of Joseph who had two extremely vivid dreams, which he shared with his family. You would hope that at least those closest to you would understand your dreams, but this is often not the reality. Joseph found this out in what seemed a very costly way. His brothers sold him into slavery and told their father that he had been killed. We see however, that God was in complete control of where Joseph's life was heading despite every injustice that he experienced.

When I was around ten years of age, my parents bought me a computer for Christmas. As I think back it almost seems crazy to call it a "computer" because our digital watches seem to have more memory these days that the unbelievable 1k that this came with. I was totally taken with it though, and used to sit for hours programming the thing to do the most pointless of tasks. You could buy magazines in those days that didn't come with disks, but with page after page of typed Basic programming that you could type, line by line, into your own computer. I loved it, particularly when it all went wrong and you had to go through the whole process of trying to understand how the program was supposed to work in order to try to correct the mistake. These early experiences with technology convinced me that I wanted to become a computer programmer when I entered the big world of work. I looked into the subjects I would need to take in school and explored the results I would need to gain from further education. My mind was made up. That was until the day when God decided that He would reveal what *He wanted me to do.*

I had gone away for a week to a Christian holiday conference in the south of England with some friends from my youth group. The holiday was actually advertised as being for 18–30s and as I was only fourteen, I was only really allowed in on the basis that others in my group were older. I was aware that I should not draw attention to myself though, so that people wouldn't make too much of me being too young.

With this in mind, on the first night I sat near the back of the opening meeting. All was going well until the guest speaker for the week got up to preach. The first thing he said was, could that guy sitting at the back please come and stand at the front? My heart began to beat faster and I began to get that sinking feeling inside, where you begin to convince yourself that you can actually taste your internal organs in your mouth! Needing a second prompting from the speaker in order to convince me that it was me he was talking to, I slowly made my way to the front, convinced that I was about to be exposed as a deceitful "under 18"! His first words to me didn't help. He said, "You are wearing aftershave, but you are not even shaving yet!" Everyone laughed as my paranoia about my "under age worship" now began to shout in my ears. What happened next blew me away. He began to prophesy into my life and the Holy Spirit came upon me and planted dreams and desires that began to create radical sparks in my life. As the tears rolled down my baby-faced cheeks, I realized that this was a meeting-with-God moment. It was a moment that remains with me to this day, because it literally changed the direction of my life. I don't think my friends saw me any differently, and I didn't see anything radically different happen on the outside, but my plans to work with computers changed to a desire to serve God. I knew that something significant had changed on the inside and that I wanted to see these dreams become a reality.

Have I seen all these dreams realized? Has the journey been one of ease and continual happiness? The answer to both is, "No". There are still many sparks within trying to catch flame. The journey so far has often been one of challenge and hard work. There have been disappointments, failures and scary moments that have been a bit hair raising (when I had some to raise that is!) But could I imagine life without the pursuit of God-given dreams? Definitely not. I believe He has not only given me the desires that are in my heart, but will also bring about the manifestation of those dreams into reality, and I want to make sure my life is committed to partnering with Him in making this possible.

Some dreams are planted in "burning bush" experiences, when God surprisingly grabs our attention and calls us to something that we weren't expecting. However, many of our dreams are planted in more subtle ways. It may be through seeing a need that we can see an answer to. It may be an inspired thought. What we do with our dreams is more important than how they are started.

He says "Yes", unless you hear otherwise

I have known people that realize they have desires and dreams in their heart that God has placed there, but they sit around hoping that one day, something is going to be different and they are going to experience their reality. One of the common hallmarks I notice in people's lives when this is the case, is a general belief that God is a bit like a race official who says, "On your marks, get set . . . ", but then takes ages to say "GO!" I've often wondered what it must feel like for a contestant on one of those TV programmes when the presenter says, "And the winner is . . . come back after the break and find out!" The studio audience groans, I groan, the goldfish groans, but that commercial break must seem like an eternity for the contestant. I have met so many people who seem to think that God says, "Come back after the break and I'll make your dreams a reality." The feeling of helplessly being in waiting can be tough, but it is a feeling that we often adopt because of a wrong view of God's inclinations.

No, Yes Yes, No?

"Dear God, You know I have this desire in my heart to start a Christian Union at my school. It seems like a good idea to my friends and me, but I pray that You will show me what Your will is." Does this prayer remind you of any you have prayed? I don't necessarily mean about starting a Christian Union! But, a prayer that asks for God to speak to you to reveal whether the desire in your heart is right to pursue. I have found that when people pray this sort of prayer, they then do nothing but wait. It's like someone placing a box of chocolates on the table in front of you and you asking if you can have one. What do you do if you get no apparent response? If you don't take one, it is because you assume that the answer is "No". And people tend to make the assumption that God generally says, "NO" unless they specifically hear Him say "YES". Consequently, they do nothing with the dreams in their heart that they have prayed about.

But what if this assumption is spun on its head? What if we live our lives based on the premise that "God says 'Yes', unless we hear Him specifically saying 'No' "? I see many characters throughout the Bible who lived this way. As I read of David picking up five stones in advance of his encounter with Goliath, I notice that there is no account of a prophetic word being given to him regarding what he was about to do. I do read that David knew he had an anointing from God and that he had built up to this moment with progressive steps of faith after first tackling a lion and then a bear. I read of the apostle Paul and his team who were stood at the border of Bithynia, wanting to enter and preach the great news about Jesus. We read that they were prevented from doing so by the Holy Spirit (Acts 16:7). They were assuming "Yes", until they heard "No". I find that these "live the dream" people, and others throughout history, who have lived their lives believing that God says "Yes" unless He says "No", are bold, courageous, adventurous and daring. They are pioneers; going where others fear to go and often seeing the reality of God's power at work in their everyday lives.

Fear of getting it wrong

If you are anything like me, then you probably are always wanting to do things right. I want to get things right. I want to please God. I want the things I do to be successful. I also believe that God wants these things for me as well, as He does for you. However, I refuse to be intimidated by the possibility that I might fail. The reality is that each time I step out for God, I may fail. Why did David pick up five stones before he attacked Goliath? Because he may have missed with the first, or the second, and so on ... Fear of failing is one of the most crippling and debilitating restraints that holds people back from pressing into their dreams. Failure shows that something is wrong and we don't want people making negative conclusions about us. For years I have been listening to stories of Peter, who stepped out of the boat and began to walk on water towards Jesus. We all know that the reason Peter fell in the water after a few successful steps was that he took his eyes of Jesus and looked at the wind (Matthew 14:29). If ever there was a public failure – this was it. Across the world, preachers regularly remind congregations of the lessons to be learnt from this incident. I have often wondered about the other disciples in the boat. For every person who steps out and takes a risk for God, there are many more who sit back and watch. Such spectators can often be experts at "sitting ministries" and will hinder those who are stepping out in faith for God – perhaps unintentionally – by either discouraging them or becoming "expert" commentators.

Discouragement

"Peter, don't be such an idiot! Sit down and help us row this boat." There will always be people who will seek to discourage us. I remember as a sixteen-year-old, desperately wanting to pursue the dreams that God had deposited in my heart. While others around me were planning their careers and doing the other usual teenage things such as learning to drive etc., I was looking into the possibilities of joining an evangelist and working as part of the team as a volunteer. There were those who tried to discourage me. One of the main discouragements I faced was being told that I was "too young". The evangelist had a real word of wisdom and told me, "If you are old enough to join the Queen's Army then you are old enough to join the King of kings' Army." If you aim to step out, there is a high possibility that others will try to discourage you. Keep sweet. Don't develop a chip on your shoulder or become cynical towards them, but do keep your eyes fixed on Jesus and don't be put off the course that you believe to be right.

Commentating

Up and down the country there are numerous armchair supporters of well-known sports. Their only regular exercise is lifting the remote control from the arm of the chair. Amazingly, they still feel that somehow they have the right and authority to comment on the ability, skill and tactics of others in a critical way. I have come in contact with many "armchair supporters" of Christian ventures. They look and listen, call themselves a supporter even, but from the comfort of their duck feather pillowed settee, they believe they know best.

I highly regard advice. I don't just appreciate it, but I regularly look for it. I believe in teams and have spent my entire ministry either working in teams or developing them. I need people around me who can lovingly disagree with me, and offer me expert thoughts on areas I'm working on. I need the accountability of leaders and friends. You need them. Your leaders are for you and you should go out of your way to respect what they say. They are either ahead of you or on the same journey of faith. Listen to these people. However, we need to beware of others who merely view the journey rather than walk it, and then insist on us heeding their advice. Don't let them side-track you. I wonder if any of the disciples did actually shout advice to Peter from the relative comfort of their boat? I cannot be sure if they did, but I can be sure that when you step out to live *your* dreams, others will shout instructions to you which could distract you from your purpose. Listen to the right people. I look to surround myself with people who are ahead of me on the journey, who I know love me enough to be honest with me if I need to be confronted. If you don't have such people around you, then pray that God would send them into your life and go looking for them.

You failed

We all love to watch those home videos that get sent in to TV shows showing things that have gone wrong. You know the ones that show the bride fainting at the altar, or the infant who pokes herself in the eye with her plastic spoon as she negotiates the art of coordinated eating in her high chair. Our culture has helped develop an instinct that enjoys other people's misfortune. I wonder how the disciples responded to the dripping wet Peter as he climbed into the boat? It has been my experience that the "told you so" crew usually surface at these moments. They seek to show you that their intellect is superior and more perceptive than yours because they knew in advance that the whole thing would end in failure. There is a smugness that oozes from them as you not only have to contend with the failure itself, but also deal with the embarrassing judgments that others are now making about you.

I would love to think that the reaction of the other disciples as Peter climbed back into the boat, was to give him a standing ovation, clapping and cheering this half-drowned man. As the applause continued, each one would come along and hug his soggy frame, saying, "Well done for giving it a go!" If we are going to create a culture that helps people to move into our God-given dreams, we must learn to honour those who have given it a go – even if they failed. Should we celebrate failure? No, but we should celebrate failures who have stepped out where others feared to tread, with the belief that they were doing this for Jesus. If we could create more "honour and encourage failure" moments in our youth groups and churches it would result in a few things:

- **Less super-spiritual justifications of things that didn't work** – We can be so bad at putting our hands up and saying we got it wrong. We usually find some clever and redemptive language to justify the venture to others. If we knew that people would accept and encourage us if we admitted failure, then I'm sure we would be more likely to be honest in this way.
- **We would learn the lessons of others** – If we were more able to share failure then we would be better placed to learn from the mistakes others have made.
- **We would create a bolder environment** – When courageous hearts are merited higher than manifest success, we create an atmosphere that fosters boldness.

What dreams and plans have you been waiting to hear God's "Yes" about? Has the fear of failing God and yourself held you back? Come on, now is not a time to sit around and be bored. Get up out of your bed and take a few risks for Jesus. Unless you hear God say "No", know that He already says "Yes". Know that He loves those who will give it a go and step out for Him. If He says "No", then stop. Otherwise, get advice, seek godly counsel, court expert opinion and go for it!

Getting out of bed

Are you going to dream the dream or are you going to live it? One will be more comfortable, but incredibly boring! The other will mean you need to move on from your past and take some risks in your present. Go on – live it! God is preparing young people for a major move of God. He is looking actively for those who will get up out of their beds and be world-changers.

The New Testament disciples were driven by a strong conviction that Jesus would be returning any day. The reason they gave everything they had to impact the nations of the world for Christ was that they believed time was running out and they had to get the job done. One of the biggest myths among young people today is that life will go on forever. Eternity will, but our life on this earth presents us with a limited window of opportunity. God is stirring the hearts of young people to be a part of the *Now generation* – a generation that will not allow the past to shackle them or the future to intimidate them. A generation that will boldly rise, full of confidence in their God, full of courage and single-minded about living out the dreams of their heart. Will you press through the barriers? Will you decide this day that nothing will hold you back and nothing will restrict you? You have the smile of God all over your life. You have the resources of heaven at your disposal. You have the opportunity to join hands with Him and walk into a new day – a day of destiny!

Contact information

To contact Serious4God email:

info@serious4god.co.uk

For more information visit:

www.serious4god.co.uk